IT Induction and
Information Security Awareness

IT Induction and Information Security Awareness
A Pocket Guide

VALERIE MADDOCK

IT Governance Publishing

FOREWORD

It's widely accepted that attention to the needs of people, process and technology is the foundation of effective information governance. Good process design and smart technology will not by themselves deliver the goods. People are the real key to successful exploitation of information and technology. People create, use and interpret data. They manage information systems and administer access rights, and they control an array of increasingly powerful desktop devices. People also make mistakes and create incidents. But at the same time, they can also identify risks, prevent incidents and respond to crises.

In everyday use of IT, it's often the people side that receives the least attention. As much as we'd like to see it, information systems are rarely built to satisfy the needs, wants and preferences of the users. The result is that few information systems are intuitive enough to be used correctly without a degree of user training. Many security risks are also invisible or counter-intuitive. It's not logical to imagine that a small, local oversight can bring down an enterprise-wide service.

Most of our business systems are reasonably well protected against physical hazards, typically running on dedicated equipment housed in secure buildings. But it only takes a single connection to an infected website, or the loss of a single memory stick, to compromise an entire database, and the damage from a major breach is often much more than just the financial cost of the incident response and investigation. It can seriously damage future revenue. Successful brands take years to establish, but their value can be quickly lost in a wave of citizen and media outrage. Constant vigilance is the price of today's freedom from breaches.

But nobody is perfect and it's often the best employees that make the biggest mistakes because they work harder, quicker and longer, and are less likely to be supervised. We cannot eliminate all accidents and errors, but we can do quite a bit to minimise the likelihood of a damaging breach. In practice, there's no such thing as an isolated incident. In the safety field, it's well known that behind every major incident there are dozens of minor incidents, hundreds of near misses and thousands of bad practices. If we can minimise those bad habits and near misses, and identify and fix the root causes of incidents, then we are much less likely to suffer a major security breach. An ounce of prevention is better than a pound of cure.

As a former security director I've often been asked: 'How big is your security function?' The true answer is: 'As big as the organisation'. In some cases I could even include the contributions of online customers. This is because information security is everyone's responsibility: from the executive board room to the reception desk. All managers and staff require regular briefings about new technologies and emerging security risks. In an increasingly networked world, where we have powerful capabilities to access data and systems across shared public networks, our collective know-how is the thin blue line that safeguards our information assets from computer intrusions and data breaches.

I'm delighted to have been asked to contribute this foreword to a practical, pocket guide. We need more educational guidance in the hands of managers, rather than in academic textbooks. I'm also a passionate believer in the power of education and awareness programmes to prevent incidents. A few years ago, when I was Director of Information Security and Risk for Royal Mail Group, I sponsored a full-time security awareness programme and I monitored its impact on security incidents. The results were staggering. I found that a single, targeted intervention could achieve a huge reduction in incident levels, by more than half in some cases. The impact of a campaign quickly fades, however. Awareness must be maintained and embedded into organisational culture to have a lasting effect.

We all need a minimum amount of awareness and training to gain the knowledge and skills needed to use systems and technology efficiently, safely and securely. Bad habits are easy to pick up and surprisingly hard to discard. And common sense is not as common as we'd like to think it might be. Training enables us to benefit from the findings and best practices of a much broader community, rather than to rely just on our own limited experience. Induction and training programmes are an essential investment for all organisations. Not only do they increase efficiency, they also help safeguard our valuable intellectual assets: the crown jewels that reside, not in bank accounts and bricks and mortar, but in our information, relationships and reputation.

David Lacey, November 2009

PREFACE

We are all on the receiving end of the rapid changes that have taken place in technology over the last two decades. These have influenced the way we communicate, how we find information and conduct research, where we store our data, and our social networking activities. Many of these technological advances have also had an impact on businesses enabling, for example, a more flexible and mobile workforce. Wireless computing is now the norm and the ever-increasing bandwidth on our broadband connections is making fixed office computing a less attractive proposition.

Equally, the myriad of small digital devices that incorporate e-mail, voice, business applications and our personal data have influenced where and how we choose to work. As we leave behind the information age and embrace the connected age we have come to expect freedom of choice in every aspect of our lives especially with regard to the way we use current technologies; hence the boundaries between our personal and working lives are disappearing.

It is not surprising then that organisations are quick to take advantage of this ubiquitous technology, and just as quickly they also experience some of the difficulties this brings, for instance, the threat of data leakage and reputational damage. As a consequence, addressing risk has become a full-time activity. Many may argue the 'fight fire with fire' approach is the easiest way to deal with information security risk by adopting the best-of-breed technology to overcome the issues that technology has enabled. The alternative approach, which is less controlling, is to educate employees in good working practice, making them aware of the risks and engendering corporate working. Neither approach is a cheap solution, but the former solution may, to some, be more attractive, not least because it is likely to be quicker.

David Lacey in his book *Managing the Human Factor in Information Security*[1] endorses the educational approach to information security, believing that empowering and trusting employees, through good educational practices and advice specific to their needs, is the best solution to address information security risk. In particular he emphasises the need for Information Security Awareness to be an ongoing activity. This pocket guide supports this approach and puts forward the case for an organisation-wide, and fully supported, IT Induction and Information Security Awareness Programme that aims to start this educational process. In particular it will provide clarity of purpose, equate the programme to organisational roles, and offer practical assistance in the development and delivery of an IT Induction programme.

---

[1] Managing the Human Factor in Information Security, Lacey D, John Wiley & Sons Ltd, Chichester (2009) ISBN 978-0-470-72199-5.

ABOUT THE AUTHOR

Valerie Maddock has over 35 years' experience in IT which started at Leeds University where she was involved in cosmic ray research analysis. Since 1975 she has been engaged in a range of information management, teaching and support roles in the public sector.

Valerie graduated from the Open University with a Computer Science degree and has since gained a Post Graduate Certificate of Education, a Diploma in eLearning Management, various Microsoft® accreditations and a Masters in Education (eLearning). She is also a Member of the British Computer Society, a Certified IT Professional and a Member of the Institute of IT Training.

She joined the IT department of The Salvation Army UK[2] in 1996 where she established an IT Learning and User Support unit to serve the organisation's growing user base, and continues in this role today. Valerie introduced IT Induction into the organisation at an early stage in her role, and her continued passion to develop flexible and innovative learning opportunities for the staff she serves has led her to develop an online IT Induction programme that best fits the changing needs of this Christian charity. As a consequence of this work, Valerie was an Individual Excellence Finalist in the BCS & Computing UK IT Industry Awards 2009 for the category IT Service and Support Professional of the Year.

---

[2] The Salvation Army is an international Christian church and charity working in 118 countries worldwide.

CONTENTS

CHAPTER 1: PUTTING IT INDUCTION IN PERSPECTIVE

Do you find the terms IT Induction and IT Introduction being used interchangeably? If yes, then it is also likely that you will have new employees in your organisation who, being IT competent, are wondering why they need to attend an IT Introduction programme, and are most likely raising objections at such a proposition. Understandably so. If you are not experiencing a conflict of these terms then you are in an enviable position.

To explain:

Introduction is about a first experience of a subject or activity, so you would expect an *IT Introduction* programme to focus on instruction on how to use IT, a skills-based training event for instance, and unlike *induction*, an introduction has a conclusion, an end point.

Induction on the other hand is less open and closed because it is educational in nature and focuses on expected behaviour as much as it does on sharing knowledge, and has little relationship to IT competencies. The aim of any induction process is to help new employees make a smooth and informed transition to their new workplace, ensuring all the basic information they need is available to them, so they are in a position to adapt quickly to their new role.

This pocket guide refers therefore to IT Induction as an educational programme or activity that informs staff within an organisation about the IT[3] facilities and services available to them, brings their attention to current IT policies and guidelines, and emphasises individual responsibilities through good working practices.

---

[3] Information and Communications Technology is implied (ICT).

So what is the relationship between IT Induction and Information Security Awareness?

Information Security is fundamentally about safeguarding information, and is based on the CIA principles:

- Confidentiality: ensuring information can only be accessed by those who are authorised to do so.
- Integrity: ensuring the information is accurate and can be trusted.
- Availability: ensuring the information is available when it is needed.

Hence, Information Security Awareness focuses on the user's responsibility, to ensure that good working practices are adopted under these broad principles, thereby reducing the likelihood to the organisation (and to some extent the individual) of legal, financial and reputational risk. Figure 1 shows how Information Security Awareness becomes an integral part of a holistic IT Induction programme.

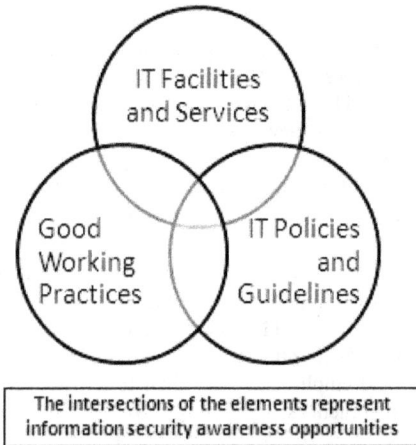

The intersections of the elements represent information security awareness opportunities

Figure 1: The relationship between the elements of an IT Induction programme and information security

From Figure 1 it can be deduced that either removing or limiting any of the elements of the IT Induction programme will have the overall effect of reducing the Information Security Awareness impact, which would not only be a missed opportunity, but may also prove to be a costly one.

How does an ICT Code of Conduct fit with IT Induction?

An employee ICT Code of Conduct or Acceptable Use Policy (AUP) is a document that sets out certain rules and guidelines that an employee is expected to follow whilst using the organisation's information systems, and will indicate what would constitute an infringement of these guidelines and the penalties of doing so. Depending on the organisation, the employee may be required to sign the Code of Conduct as part of their employee contract or before being given access to the organisation's information systems. Consequently, the ICT Code of Conduct sits within the IT Policies and Guidelines element of IT Induction, as shown in Figure 1, and is therefore an integral part of the programme. It would thus make logical sense for a new employee to undertake the IT Induction programme prior to signing the Code of Conduct, as this will give the document more significance.

In summary, this chapter has distinguished between IT Introduction and IT Induction. It has indicated three key content areas for the IT Induction programme, and shown how these overlap to bring about integral Information Security Awareness opportunities into the programme.

CHAPTER 2: THE TARGET AUDIENCE

Generally, organisations provide an induction for all new employees, and this may be a generic programme or tailored to meet job profiles. As this pocket guide is focusing on IT Induction, does this change the target audience, and should IT Induction be specific to job profiles?

Certainly there is a valid argument that tailoring an induction programme to specific roles is likely to be more effective than a generic stance, although more time-consuming and potentially more expensive to develop and deliver. For instance, there may be a number of specialist IT roles in your organisation, including staff in the IT department, who would benefit from a customised IT Induction; however, it may also be your view that this approach may be too detailed and excessive for your organisational requirements, or could be managed by an alternative route.

Assuming, for practicality purposes, a generic IT Induction programme is planned, it would seem reasonable to assume that the target audience for this programme would be any new employee who requires access to the organisation's information systems, also known as a 'new user'. This compares with an employee induction, where it is unlikely that anyone would be excluded from this knowledge-sharing activity.

Having established the target audience for the IT Induction programme let us now explore the types of new users you may encounter in your organisation.

A new user is generally understood to be an employee who has just taken up an appointment in the organisation. The Human Resources (HR) department will know of this individual as a consequence of recruitment and payroll tasks, and the new employee would have been identified as requiring access to the organisation's information systems resulting from their job role. Alternatively, a new user may be an employee who does not currently have access to the organisation's information systems, but now requires access as a result of a change in their job role or circumstances.

Should you assume then that your senior executives would come under the same definition of a new user if they require access to the organisation's information systems? If so, you would expect them to undertake the IT Induction in much the same way as any new employee. Whilst there is always an exception to any rule, gaining senior executive buy-in to an IT Induction programme is paramount. Not only does this present a professional and responsible image of the organisation from the top, why wouldn't a senior member of staff want to know the 'messages' that were being given to their employees? If this generic approach to IT Induction proves unachievable at executive level, then a more role- based adaptation of the IT Induction will need to be forthcoming at the very least.

Are there any other types of new user in your organisation? For instance, do you employ temporary or contract staff that require system access? If so, should these staff be required to complete the IT Induction programme? Most definitely.

Temporary and contract staff, as these terms suggest, are often short-term workers, and either work independently or associate themselves more closely with a third party company. Therefore they present, potentially, a greater risk to your information security than a long-term employee. This is not to suggest that third party staff are any the less professional or less committed to your organisation, but to state a fact of less permanency and potentially more multi-organisation working.

In some organisations, facilitating IT Induction for temporary staff can often to lead contention, and this may be a direct result of managers not fully appreciating the importance of the IT Induction programme. It is understandable that the cost per day for a temporary or contract worker might be uppermost in the mind of a manager when asked to release staff for an IT Induction activity, especially if the staff involved are employed on a very short- term contract, and the manager still hasn't managed to distinguish between IT Introduction and IT Induction.

Think of it this way, if a worker, regardless of their employment status, is not provided with a relevant IT Induction it is like giving them the keys to your much-loved car, even though you know they have no knowledge or understanding of the Highway Code. This may be OK, as long as you only want them to drive up and down your farm track.

Many of you reading this pocket guide may have had the opportunity to discuss with temporary staff or contract workers how they feel about being asked to complete an IT Induction. If so, I hope you had a similar response to me in that these staff are quite used to working in a variety of organisations, experiencing a wide range of induction-type procedures, and they both expect and welcome an IT and employee-type induction.

There is another category of staff that may cause a problem with regard to compliance with IT Induction – volunteer workers. Charities in particular welcome the extra resource provided by volunteer workers. However, volunteer workers, irrespective of their charitable endeavours, present a number of challenges to an organisation, and providing access to the organisation's information systems is just one of these. Unlike third party staff, who have a contract in place, many volunteers work on a completely different basis, and the potential information security risk for a freelance person with no contract or terms of engagement, irrespective of their abilities and professionalism, should not be underestimated or ignored. Assessing risk is out of scope for this pocket guide; however, it is clear that volunteers are most definitely candidates for the IT Induction programme.

In summary, this chapter has put forward that IT Induction is for everyone, from the chief executive, or equivalent, through to volunteer staff, if any of these roles require them to have access to the organisation's information systems. The next chapter will address who is responsible for making IT Induction happen for these staff.

CHAPTER 3: WHOSE RESPONSIBILITY IS IT ANYWAY?

Who is responsible for employee education in your organisation? The responsibility often lies within the HR department or a separate Learning and Development unit. However, it is not unknown to have subject matter experts scattered across the organisation that have individual educational responsibilities. And, increasingly, learning and development is outsourced to third party organisations.

Quite frankly, it doesn't really matter who has the responsibility, as long as employee education happens. This does not imply that the relevance and quality of the educational programmes are not important, but to simply underline the fact that someone, somewhere, has to have a recognised responsibility for the development and delivery of specific employee education. So, who would or should have the responsibility for the IT Induction programme? This really depends on your organisation and where the subject matter expertise resides.

Let us first consider the subject matter-expertise that is required to develop an IT Induction programme. Firstly, the subject matter expert should have a fundamental understanding of the organisation's IT infrastructure. This just means having an overall understanding of the platforms used across the organisation and how they connect, so the subject-matter expert can relate this to the type of services that the infrastructure will deliver to the users, for example, mobile or flexible working opportunities. Secondly, the subject matter expert should be knowledgeable about the software used on these platforms. Again, this does not imply having expertise in using this software, but to understand the services and facilities offered to the user through the software strategy adopted by the organisation. Thirdly, the subject matter expert needs to know about the range of web-based resources available to the users and whether any of these are restricted to certain user groups or restricted by location. Fourthly, the subject matter expert needs to be fully aware of what constitutes good IT working practice and have a good knowledge of information security issues. Finally, and perhaps most important of all, they need to know the users. So who is this subject matter expert? Is it the IT director, a senior IT technician, the information security officer, an IT trainer, an IT representative, an HR specialist or a risk manager? And, does it have to be one person? You will know the answer to these questions based on your organisation structure and staff expertise, and it may well be a third party responsibility in your organisation. Irrespective of who is most suited to this task, their commitment to developing and maintaining the IT Induction programme will be key to the effectiveness of the programme you adopt.

What has not been addressed here is who will have the skills to deliver the IT Induction programme. A well-informed IT Induction development deserves expert delivery, thereby increasing the probability of a memorable experience for the user, leaving them in no doubt about the IT systems available to them, codes of practice and expected behaviour. This is the focus of Chapter 5 which will address the various methods of delivery to help you decide which approach would most suit your organisation.

Having established that a certain amount of IT expertise is required along with a good knowledge of your users to develop and deliver an IT Induction programme, does this imply that the responsibility for IT Induction is unlikely to sit within your HR department or equivalent body? The Chartered Institute of Personnel and Development[4] state that the role of HR is to ensure an induction policy is in place, and the role of HR professionals is to oversee the development and availability of induction programmes and evaluate their effectiveness. Would this exclude IT Induction? Perhaps not. In practice, it is likely that the development and delivery of IT Induction would be delegated to experts outside the HR

------

[4] *www.cipd.co.uk/subjects/recruitmen/induction/induction.htm*

department. Nevertheless HR, or your equivalent, will still retain overall responsibility for the induction of new employees, including IT aspects of this, as induction is a necessary undertaking for the management of personnel.

Does this leave the chief executive officer off the hook with regard to IT Induction? Whichever management book you have read, and for whatever purpose, it is certain that there will have been mention, if not a dedicated chapter, on the importance of senior management buy-in, a sponsor for your cause or support from the executive board. Why should IT Induction be any different? After all, it is the point at which an impression is made with new staff and standards are set. And who will be legally responsible for any mishaps? Who would have the most to lose? Whilst you would not expect senior staff to get involved in the detail of an IT Induction programme, unless they are especially impassioned by the topic, you should expect them to understand information security risk at a high level, and support any effort to educate users in reducing risk within the organisation. The detail can be left to the experts they employ. Nevertheless, undertaking the IT Induction programme themselves and expecting all other staff to do the same is the standard you want them to set.

Question
You joined the organisation four weeks ago as a financial administrator. To date, neither the HR department nor your line manager has offered you any information on IT, associated policies, procedures and employee-expected behaviour. Do you:

A. Say nothing. Being glad you got away with it, as these things are so boring and badly done.

B. Mention it to a colleague over coffee, as you may be missing something.

C. Approach your line manager and ask for assistance in getting access to relevant information and people who can fill in the gaps.

D. Go to HR and complain that the organisation is putting you and them at risk, and they really should do something about IT Induction.

Choice A is simply not an option. IT Induction is the responsibility of everyone.

Choice B is a start, assuming your colleague can help by giving you some background information. However, their understanding may be out of date or even prejudicial, so you would need to be able to keep yourself detached from any harboured resentment or bad habits.

Choice C is a better approach as your line manager should be expected to ensure that you have received the required employee induction. This does assume your line manager is conversant and supportive of any IT Induction process in operation.

Choice D will probably depend on your charm and gift for communication, as complaining to HR so early in your appointment may not be a good move. However, you should expect to find out if there is an IT Induction, and if so, how you can access the programme. If there is no specific IT Induction, then at the very least you need to know where to find IT user policy and guidelines. Did you receive or sign an Acceptable Use Policy document? Also, do you think as an end user you have the responsibility to draw attention to the risk of not providing adequate IT Induction for all users? I would say so.

What this question aims to reinforce is that all staff should have the opportunity to undertake IT Induction and Information Security Awareness, education, and it is everyone's responsibility to make sure this happens.

In summary, this chapter has explored who should develop an IT Induction programme, and where the responsibility lies for ensuring IT Induction reaches all new users. Whilst a number of specific roles have been identified regarding IT Induction development and for taking the responsibility for ensuring IT Induction happens, it is clear that neither senior executives nor the end user are excluded from this responsibility.

CHAPTER 4: INDICATIVE CONTENT

Having established the case and audience for IT induction, this chapter will look into the programme in more detail, suggesting content that you may adopt or adapt to your own organisational needs. At this point, it often helps to be reminded of the aim of the programme. For example:

To inform system users of: the IT facilities and services that are available to them; current IT policies and guidelines; and to endorse individual responsibilities and working practices whilst using the organisation's information systems.

How can we now turn this into practical content? It is probably easier to imagine yourself as a new user in the organisation. So typically you might want to know how to gain access to the information system(s), what resources you will have available, and if there is anything you specifically should, or should not, do whilst using the system(s).

The following provides a number of broad headings to help you get started and are not intended to be definitive.

System access

The new user will probably want to know:

- Their username and password.
- The password policy; for instance, the strength of passwords, and how and when they should change their password.

The organisation may also want them to know:

- That the Acceptable Use Policy is in operation once they gain access to the organisation's information systems.
- Organisational policy or guidelines on constructing and remembering passwords, and who to turn to for help when they forget their passwords or discover a need to share resources protected by passwords. It may help to observe user behaviour with regard to password management, for instance if 'sticky notes' decorate monitors with reminders, does this habit also include jotting down usernames and passwords? Paperless offices may not have this problem; however, could the digital equivalent present similar risks?
- How to secure active network sessions when the user needs to be away from their computer.
- About any 'lock out' policy that is in place.

For instance, after being unsuccessful at gaining access to the system on three attempts, does the system lock the user out, considering them to be a threat? If so, the user will need to know what they have to do to unlock their account.

System resources

Once a new user has gained access to the system they will probably want to know:

- The desktop productivity tools that will be available to them. For instance, does the organisation provide Microsoft® Office? If so, what version and which applications?
- The organisational policy on gaining access to non-standard applications and specific corporate systems.

- The file storage facilities they have, and whether there is a standard filing structure and limits to the file store.
- About IT training and support provision. If these services are available, how can they access this resource or service?

The organisation may also want them to know:

- That unauthorised access to system resources is subject to the Computer Misuse Act 1990.
- That personal information that can identify a living individual is subject to the Data Protection Act 1998, and to inform the user who has the role of Data Protection Officer within the organisation.
- Organisational policy on transferring data from the system to a portable storage device. For example, what is the policy on USB memory stick use?
- Organisational policy or guidelines on bringing data into internal systems from an external location, including anti-virus policy or guidelines.
- Organisational policy or guidelines on sharing data storage locations and collaborative working arrangements.
- Organisational policy on the use of spreadsheets to model or store corporate data.
- Organisational printer policy. This may include eco-friendly printer use, confidential printing and overall good practice.
- Any associated clear desk policies or recommendations to support data confidentiality.

Connectivity

More common these days is the requirement for users to mix and match their home and work environments, including using their personal equipment. Whilst some organisations have clear and indisputable policies on this, others may not.

A new user may want to know:

- Whether they can use their own personal computer equipment, either on or off the organisation's network, including their use of mobile phones, PDAs or personal printers.
- The telephone systems that are in use, how to get help in using them, and whether they can synchronise their personal and work contacts through the systems provided.

The organisation may also want them to know:

- Organisational policy or guidelines for home and mobile working.
- Whether taking personal calls during working hours, or in certain working environments, is permitted or restricted.
- How to physically secure their mobile equipment.

E-mail

It is generally a given that all users will be provided with an e-mail account to conduct their business. Although hard to imagine in today's connected society, there may be a few exceptions where the user's role in the organisation will exclude this facility.

Most organisations will have their own domain names and e-mail systems. This provides more security for communication and endorses the corporate brand, and should therefore prompt good working practice guidelines.

The new user will probably want to know:

- Their internal and external e-mail address.
- The e-mail system that the organisation uses, and how they can get help in using it.
- Details of standard distribution groups or mailing lists.

The organisation may also want them to know:

- Privacy expectations.
- About any e-mail storage quotas in operation.
- About general or specific netiquette rules, especially with regard to corporate brand and communication policies.
- The organisational policy or guidelines on whether they are allowed to send personal e- mail from their business e-mail address.
- Whether accessing their personal e-mail from work is permissible or restricted to certain times, for instance to coincide with lunch breaks.
- Instant Messaging facilities and restrictions if appropriate.
- About how the ubiquitous nature of e-mail often presents itself as an informal form of communication and therefore to remind users that contracts can be made or broken via e- mail, and also that the contents of an e-mail can be used in litigation.
- That should the content of an e-mail identify a living individual, then it may be subject to the Data Protection Act 1998.
- That an e-mail sent, accessed or altered by an individual masquerading as someone else is illegal and subject to the Computer Misuse Act 1990.
- About any restrictions on sending and receiving file attachments, including compatibility issues between software versions, and practical tips on how to avoid these.

- The threats from phishing scams and spam attacks and what mechanisms the organisation has in place to reduce these threats. The new user should know through IT Induction, initially, how to handle these types of e-mail threats, and equally be aware of the consequences of being a perpetrator of such communication malpractice.

Web facilities

Increasingly, organisations have internal and external web-based systems, which may have restricted or controlled access. The IT Induction programme is an ideal opportunity to inform the users of web resources that are available to everyone, and where to find out about restricted resources, if appropriate.

The new user will probably want to know:

- How to access any intranet and/or extranet the organisation has, and who has content responsibilities.
- About the organisation's public website and who is responsible for its content (although this is often discovered in preparation for the interview).
- Whether the organisation has any collaborative or social networking sites. If so, where to find out about the rules of engagement.

The organisation may also want them to know:

- What is permissible regarding personal surfing and e-commerce, and perhaps a brief caveat on international law in this respect.
- Details about any web filtering that is in place.
- Good practice guidelines on accessing multimedia via the Internet.

- The user's responsibilities relating to the Copyright, Designs and Patents Act 1988.
- What is permissible and appropriate regarding downloading of materials and the increasing threat from malicious software.
- The importance of corporate branding, and where to find out about marketing and branding information.
- The issues for the individual and the organisation that may result as a consequence of providing personal or business details on public websites.

Health and safety

Generally, new staff don't have this item on their agenda, assuming modern office equipment will meet all health and safety requirements. However, they should be reminded of what they can expect the organisation to provide for them, and what the employer will expect from them in terms of how they use the equipment provided. This is quite clearly described in The Health and Safety at Work Act 1994.[5]

IT services

It is helpful to inform new users as to whether the organisation has an IT department and, if so, the services it provides.

The new user will probably want to know:
- How to contact the Service Desk (aka User Support or Help Desk) and their hours of operation.

The organisation may also want them to know:

---

[5] *www.hse.gov.uk/legislation/hswa.htm.*

- Whether Service Desk is a single point of contact for all IT enquiries; if so, the contact details should appear regularly throughout the IT Induction material. Alternatively, you will want the new users to know what IT services are available and how to access them.

Whilst this chapter has suggested appropriate content for an IT Induction programme, it is important to keep both the content and its level of detail in perspective. A lengthy and detailed IT Induction is likely to be overwhelming for a new user and unlikely to be memorable. Conversely, a brief IT Induction may leave the new user with too many questions rather than answers, which will not only result in frustration but could also create a poor first impression. Getting the content just right is not always easy, and one way to judge what is needed is to exercise reflective practice through evaluations, observations and talking to users. Service Desk experience can also provide some valuable insight into users' difficulties or lack of understanding, all of which should then be used to refine the IT Induction programme.

Recommended Reading

Data Protection Compliance in the UK, Jay R and Clarke J, IT Governance Publishing Ltd (2008) ISBN: 9781905356492.

IT Regulatory Compliance in the UK today, Calder A, IT Governance Publishing Ltd (2007) ISBN: 9781905356270.

Also visit the following websites:

The Information Commissioner's website at
www.ico.gov.uk.

The Office of Public Sector Information at
www.opsi.gov.uk.

CHAPTER 5: DELIVERY OPTIONS

Having decided on the content for your IT Induction, you will then need to decide on the best way to communicate this information to your new users. The method of delivery you choose will depend on your organisation, the facilities and resources you have available and certain characteristics of your new users. Some of the factors to consider in choosing the delivery method(s) may include:

- Number of staff involved.
- Geographical location of users.
- Staff availability; for instance do staff work shift patterns?
- Availability of relevant teaching/subject matter expertise.
- Time restrictions on the learning.
- Flexibility expectations.
- How often the information will need to be updated.
- Budget.
- Accessibility issues.
- The organisation's stance on environmental issues.

A comparison of training delivery methods is shown in Table 1.

Table 1 Comparison of Common Delivery Methods

	On the job	Printed material	Classroom	Online course	Online tutorial
Audience size	1:1	1:many	1:<10	1:many	1:many but may be restricted
Staff location	Staff dependent	Location independent	Tutor/staff dependent	Location independent	Location independent
Tutor knowledge	Local expert dependent	Subject matter expertise captured	Tutor dependent	Subject matter expertise captured	Tutor dependent
Pace	User driven	User driven	Tutor driven	User driven	Tutor driven

	On the job	Printed material	Classroom	Online course	Online tutorial
Clarification opportunities (Q&A)	Immediate	Not immediate	Immediate	Not immediate	Potentially immediate
Role specific	Yes	Likely to be generic, but has potential for role relevance	Likely to be generic, but has potential for role relevance depending on staff mix	Likely to be generic, but has potential for role relevance	Likely to be generic, but has potential for role relevance depending on staff mix
Suitability for shift workers	Depends on availability of local expert	Yes	No	Yes	No
Consistency of material and delivery	No	Yes	No	Yes	No
Currency of knowledge	Depends on the local expert	Not immediate. Would require versioning and redistribution	Tutor dependent	Not immediate. Would require updating and republishing	Tutor dependent

	On the job	Printed material	Classroom	Online course	Online tutorial
Repeatability	Depends on the local expert	Yes	Only by attending the session again	Yes	If recorded
Assessment	Subjective, but potential for objective assessment	Fairly restricted	Subjective, but potential for objective assessment	Objective	Subjective, but potential for objective assessment
Training audit	Depends on the local expert	No	Tutor dependent	Yes	Tutor dependent
Cost	Staff time (every event)	Development and distribution (once only depending on updates)	Staff/tutor time, potentially supply staff, venue, travelling & accommodation (every event)	Development and hosting (once only depending on updates)	Staff/tutor time and hosting (every event)
Accessibility	Easier to accommodate in a 1:1 situation	May need a Braille or large print version	Could prove difficult to accommodate in a mixed staff group	Would need to be developed according to accessibility guidelines	Could prove challenging
Eco-friendly	Yes	No	No	Yes	Yes

The characteristics of each training method outlined in Table 1 should help you decide which training approach would most suit your organisation and your users. Particularly where the users are concerned, you may want to take cognisance of their preferred learning style. However, in reality, this proves quite difficult to realise, especially if you have a large and diverse user population. There is also a counter-argument to learning styles in that users who are only able to learn in one style limit their educational opportunities as they will become selective in what they learn based on how the learning is delivered.

Nevertheless, the methods that have been outlined in Table 1, can be successfully combined into a learning programme resulting in a blended learning approach, which may provide for a more flexible solution. Notwithstanding these flexible learning opportunities, the maintainability of the IT Induction programme is key to its success and therefore any chosen delivery solution must be one that can be consistently supported by the organisation. Chapter 7 discusses further the maintainability of the IT Induction programme.

CHAPTER 6: MAKING IT INDUCTION PART OF A NEW USER PROCESS

At this stage in the IT Induction journey you are now ready to share IT Induction with your users, and regardless of how you have decided to deliver this knowledge, which was discussed in Chapter 5, how can you ensure that all your target audience participate in the programme?

It will certainly help if you have gained approval from senior management to make IT Induction a mandatory activity for a new starter. However, if this proves too difficult to achieve in the short term, then having an optional IT Induction programme is far better than not having one at all. Before accepting these *faits accomplis*, consider the approach, adopted by The Salvation Army UK.

Case study

The IT department of The Salvation Army UK has wide-ranging responsibilities including information security. They also have their own IT Learning unit which is teamed with User Support. The IT Learning unit has the responsibility for enabling staff IT competency, education and knowledge sharing. Consequently, the HR department have separated the responsibility for IT Induction from employee induction, endorsing both the subject matter expertise and teaching skills within the IT department, and therefore the IT department have the responsibility for IT Induction and Information Security Awareness in its entirety.

The IT Learning unit redesigned their classroom- based IT Induction programme to bring it up to date and also to make it available online. Consequently, all new users located anywhere in the UK were able to access *IT Induction Online*.

To ensure IT Induction and Information Security were taken seriously, they gained support from the leadership of the organisation to make IT Induction a mandatory undertaking. Given their partnership with User Support, they then devised a process by which all new accounts were put on hold until the IT Induction had been successfully completed. Successful completion was defined as working through the online material and answering at least 70% of the knowledge questions correctly. The tracking system they employed enabled them to check staff progress and therefore sanction release of the user accounts accordingly. Staff who are unable to meet the success criteria are coached and supported as appropriate, although this remains a rare occurrence.

Paradoxically, to access *IT Induction Online*, the new user requires a network account, but their account is on hold pending successful completion of the IT Induction. This impasse is resolved by the provision of a unique IT Induction account which enables the new user to use the organisation's network to access *IT Induction Online*, but which prevents them from accessing any other system resource.

IT Induction Online is also published as a private secure website, making it available to any new starter with Internet access. At the log-in page of the IT Induction programme they use personalised log-in credentials, provided by IT Learning, to gain full access to the programme and this enables their individual progress to be recorded.

All temporary and contract staff are also subject to the same process and procedure. As a consequence of the programme being available from any Internet connection, they are able to choose when and where they complete the programme, even from home, therefore enabling them to start work as soon as possible.

And the result?

IT Induction Online was launched in the summer of 2008, and around 50 new users a month have undertaken the programme since then. Following an evaluation of these users during September 2009, when a proportional representation of Salvation Army staff expressed their views about the programme, the following results were revealed:

- 90% of the staff understood the necessity for IT Induction.
- 80% indicated *IT Induction Online* had some influence on their working practices (13% reported a large influence).
- 97% reported it was very easy to access and navigate.
- 76% reported the content was easy to follow.
- 63% reported the knowledge questions helped them quite a lot to further their understanding of the content.
- 75% rated the experience as 'Very Good' or 'Excellent'.
- The majority of the users spent between 30 and 60 minutes working through the programme.

Furthermore, the results showed that making the course mandatory had not caused any real issues with staff and they viewed the process as a quick and easy solution. They acknowledged the vast improvement over face-to-face or telephone training and the flexibility that enabled them to undertake the programme at any time, which was particularly valued by shift workers.

In addition, User Support fully endorsed the process, and the Service Desk tools they used enabled effective logging and delegation of new user set-up tasks, which included the IT Induction element of the user account process.

The evaluation results also reported that 36% of the staff would be prepared to revisit *IT Induction Online* especially if the material was updated. This suggests that IT Induction should not be viewed as a one time only experience and is the subject of the final chapter in this pocket guide.

For further information contact: Valerie Maddock
Head of IT Learning & User Support
The Salvation Army UK
valerie.maddock@salvationarmy.org.uk.

CHAPTER 7: IT INDUCTION – A ONE TIME ONLY EXPERIENCE

Throughout this pocket guide there has been the suggestion that IT Induction is a one time only experience for new users. However, if the content of your IT Induction goes beyond informing users of file storage locations, and has a good information security element, it is worth considering ways in which users could revisit IT Induction, in so doing reinforcing user responsibilities and good working practice. Here are four scenarios where revisiting the IT Induction may be appropriate in your organisation:

- Revisiting the IT Induction could be timed around staff annual appraisals, and you may even consider making this an essential part of the appraisal process.

- Opportunities to encourage, or mandate, a revisit to IT Induction may arise in situations where staff are moving from one location in the organisation to another, especially if the IT platform or facilities are different.

- IT Induction would benefit those staff who have returned to work from a long period of absence, for instance maternity leave, or long- term sick leave, and it may be opportune to mandate this prior to re-initiating their user account.

- It is a sad fact that in any organisation there will be staff who defy organisational policy and procedure or take advantage of the IT systems. In these circumstances, especially where the misdeed is not too serious, an insistence on revisiting the IT Induction and Information Security Awareness programme may be an apt outcome.

These scenarios suggest IT Induction is not really meant to be a one time only experience for users. But what about those involved in its development; is it a one time only experience for them? To answer this question let us revisit the diagram introduced in Chapter 1, which is reproduced below.

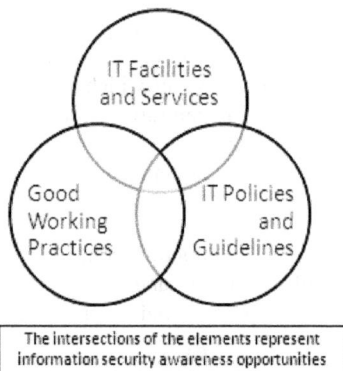

The intersections of the elements represent information security awareness opportunities

Figure 2: The relationship between the elements of an IT Induction programme and information security

It seems unlikely that any one of these elements will remain static over time. For example, a change in IT service provision, for instance, enabling or disabling the use of USB storage devices, will necessarily have an impact on IT Policy and Guidelines and working practice recommendations, all of which will have an impact on information security, which you may recall from Chapter 1 revolves around the confidentiality, integrity and availability of your data.

Therefore, given the dynamic IT environment in which most of us work and live, those involved in the development of IT Induction and Information Security Awareness programmes should expect to revisit the programme on a regular basis to ensure it is still fit for purpose, whilst tutors will be required to keep their knowledge and understanding current, if they are charged with the responsibility of disseminating this information.

In summary, it is important to remember that IT Induction and Information Security Awareness is about keeping your organisation's data safe, protecting personal data and safeguarding the organisation's brand through educating your users not only in good IT working practices but also in encouraging organisation-wide responsibility. To achieve this, your IT Induction and Information Security Awareness programme must be accessible, relevant and up to date, and for these reasons alone it is unlikely to be a one time only experience for the author, or the recipients of the programme.

ITG RESOURCES

IT Governance Ltd. sources, creates and delivers products and services to meet the real-world, evolving IT governance needs of today's organisations, directors, managers and practitioners. The ITG website (*www.itgovernance.co.uk*) is the international one-stop-shop for corporate and IT governance information, advice, guidance, books, tools, training and consultancy. *www.itgovernance.co.uk/it-induction-and-information- security.aspx* is the information page from our website for these resources.

Other Websites

Books and tools published by IT Governance Publishing (ITGP) are available from all business booksellers and are also immediately available from the following websites:

www.itgovernance.co.uk/catalog/355 provides information and online purchasing facilities for every currently available book published by ITGP.

www.itgovernanceusa.com is a US$-based website that delivers the full range of IT Governance products to North America, and ships from within the continental US.

www.itgovernanceasia.com provides a selected range of ITGP products specifically for customers in South Asia.

www.27001.com is the IT Governance Ltd. website that deals specifically with information security management, and ships from within the continental US.

Pocket Guides

For full details of the entire range of pocket guides, simply follow the links at *www.itgovernance.co.uk/publishing.aspx*.
Toolkits

ITG's unique range of toolkits includes the IT Governance Framework Toolkit, which contains all the tools and guidance that you will need in order to develop and implement an appropriate IT governance framework for your organisation. Full details can be found at *www.itgovernance.co.uk/products/519*.

For a free paper on how to use the proprietary CALDER- MOIR IT Governance Framework, and for a free trial version of the toolkit, see *www.itgovernance.co.uk/calder_moir.aspx*.

There is also a wide range of toolkits to simplify implementation of management systems, such as an ISO/IEC 27001 ISMS or a BS25999 BCMS, and these can all be viewed and purchased online at: *www.itgovernance.co.uk/catalog/1*.

Best Practice Reports

ITG's range of Best Practice Reports is now at *www.itgovernance.co.uk/best-practice-reports.aspx*. These offer you essential, pertinent, expertly researched information on an increasing number of key issues including Web 2.0 and Green IT.

Training and Consultancy

IT Governance also offers training and consultancy services across the entire spectrum of disciplines in the information governance arena. Details of training courses can be accessed at *www.itgovernance.co.uk/training.aspx* and descriptions of our consultancy services can be found at *www.itgovernance.co.uk/consulting.aspx*. Why not contact us to see how we could help you and your organisation?

Newsletter

IT governance is one of the hottest topics in business today, not least because it is also the fastest moving, so what better way to keep up than by subscribing to ITG's free monthly newsletter *Sentinel*? It provides monthly updates and resources across the whole spectrum of IT governance subject matter, including risk management, information security, ITIL and IT service management, project governance, compliance and so much more. Subscribe for your free copy at: *www.itgovernance.co.uk/newsletter.aspx*.

EU for product safety is Stephen Evans, The Mill Enterprise Hub, Stagreenan, Drogheda, Co. Louth, A92 CD3D, Ireland. (servicecentre@itgovernance.eu)